A leader's guide to
WHO IS *MY* MONEY IMPORTANT TO?

King James Bible References.

An Equanimity: Eclipse Enlightenment LLC.
Publication.

P.O. Box #3962
Brandon, FL. 33509

CHARLES H. BOXSLEY JR.

It is important to emphasize that the information in this book is solely intended to awaken and inspire the entrepreneurial spirit in those who read its content. This is not a financial solve-all publication. You should consult financial experts for advice concerning your unique situation. The author and publisher disclaim any liabilities obtained while utilizing the contents of this book.

A leader's guide to
WHO IS MY MONEY IMPORTANT TO?

ISBN: 979-8-9985776-1-1
King James Bible References
An Equanimity: Eclipse Enlightenment LLC. Publication.
P.O. Box #3962
Brandon, FL. 33509

Printed in the United States

Table of Contents

Foreword..v

Introduction..1

Chapter 1
Father Knows Best..11

Chapter 2
Even Satan Prays..25

Chapter 3
Say Uncle..35

Chapter 4
My Creditors..47

Chapter 5
My Money?..57

Reflections..69

WHO IS MY MONEY IMPORTANT TO?

Foreword

By Dominique White-Boxsley-- *Financial Literacy Educator, Loan Officer, Advocate for Purpose-Driven Living*

Have you ever looked at your bank account and wondered, "Why can't I seem to get ahead, no matter how hard I work?" Have you ever felt like your money had a mind of its own—disappearing as quickly as it came, always slipping through your fingers?

If so, you're not alone—and this book may be the breakthrough you've been waiting for.

In these pages, you'll find something rare: a brutally honest, deeply personal, and spiritually anchored approach to understanding your relationship with money. This is not a dry financial guide full of formulas and jargon. It's not about crypto, quick riches, or complex stock charts.

This book is about you—your mindset, your habits, your spiritual grounding and your inner capacity to change your financial trajectory.

What makes this book powerful is that it doesn't just talk to you, it speaks for you. ***Charles H. Boxsley Jr.***, the author of this transformative work, knows what it means to live in financial chaos, to make mistake after mistake and to wonder if lasting stability is even possible. But he also knows what it means to break free from that cycle—and he wants the same for you.

You'll read stories that hit close to home: about repossessed cars, unpaid bills, bounced checks and financial shame. But you'll also find hope—real, practical hope that comes from learning how to rebuild from the inside out.

Through biblical principles, personal testimony and practical steps, ***Charles H. Boxsley Jr.*** shows that financial recovery isn't about how much you make—it's about how well you understand the rules of the money game and how intentional you are about playing to win.

So Why Should You Buy This Book?

- **Because it will challenge you**—to stop blaming others and start building systems that serve you.
- **Because it will equip you**—with practical, action-based tools to move from surviving to thriving.
- **Because it will inspire you**—to see that you are not too far gone, too old or too broken to change your story.
- **Because it will remind you**—that God cares about your money and that purpose and provision are connected.
- **Because it will teach you**—how to create value the world will pay for.

- and how to stop working just to stay broke.

This is a book you won't just read once. You'll return to it every time you hit a wall, every time you need a reminder that your financial breakthrough isn't a fantasy, it's a decision away.

Whether you're drowning in debt, living paycheck to paycheck or simply looking to reset your financial habits once and for all, this book by ***Charles H. Boxsley Jr.*** is your wake-up call and your roadmap.

It's time to stop sleeping on your potential. It's time to take ownership. It's time to answer the question that sits at the core of this book:

"Is your money important to you?"

If you're ready to stop surviving and start sowing toward a better future, turn the page. Let's begin the journey together.

INTRODUCTION

Arise Sleepy-Head

There are truths in the Bible about God's view of you—and your money—that you may not know. I was shocked to learn that we are all born into this world spiritually asleep until something—or someone—shakes us awake.

If you love to sleep and someone tries to rouse you, your instinct might be to slap, punch, or resist with all your might. But light sleepers? They'll stir subconsciously and begin moving, if only slightly, toward the right direction at the very first glimpse of light.

When someone shakes you, your first question is likely, *"What time is it?"* That question signals a deeper desire: to know how long you've been asleep—unaware of what's really happening around you. You're not angry about being shaken; instead, you spring into action, rushing to realign yourself with the level of purpose and progress you now realize you've missed.

Each accomplishment from that point forward is like waking up more and more from a dreamlike existence—one that was drifting toward mediocrity, at best. You would realize, like I did, you've been living in a dream world which appeared to be real.

The Seed...Inside and Out

Eventually, everyone has their day of shaking. This moment comes when someone challenges your lack of progress in an area of your life, forcing you to reflect honestly on your past choices. What they say may feel offensive, but that confrontation becomes a mirror—a tool for self-awareness. This is your moment of shaking.

This is now your day of shaking. Your spirit— the truest part of you—is being summoned. It's time to make your spiritual life your priority. The person you've dressed up and presented to the world has been living in a dream. I had to face this truth about myself, and now so must you. This is your moment to wake up.

A shadow doesn't move on its own—it only moves when the object moves first. The shadow is a reflection of the real thing. In the same way, we're living in a shadow world, while a higher reality exists beyond what we see. You are not a body that happens to have a spirit. You are a spirit which happens to have a body.

Like a seed that must be planted, the outer shell is simply a protective covering—it holds no lasting value. What truly matters is inside.

Within the seed lies power, purpose, and potential that can nourish both itself and others. From within, an outward pressure builds and pushes to be released. That pressure contains gifts and self-motivating forces designed to help you fulfill your God-given purpose.

I had to engraft this into my reasoning, and now I challenge you to do the same.

Let's go just a little deeper. Your spirit is driven by words. Some words are life-giving; others bring decay. Life-giving words uplift, strengthen and edify. Negative words tear down, discourage and destroy.

Because words are alive, they *move*. Yes—they literally move because they carry spiritual energy. The more positive, truth-filled words you consume, the clearer your spiritual vision becomes.

Like Gold Around Babies

Now I'm going to say a few things, just let them settle in your heart. Don't feel like you need to. fully understand it all right away. Sometimes, we must wash a garment multiple times to get all the stains out. Let these words continue to work on you.

As you grow more excited about your spiritual journey, don't get discouraged when others fail to share your enthusiasm. It's like finding a piece of gold among a group of babies.

Imagine your excitement—you'd polish that gold, admire its shine, and want to tell everyone about your discovery. But not everyone wants gold. Some people prefer pacifiers. Why? Because gold has no value to them. Give a baby the choice between a piece of gold and a pacifier, and they'll choose the gold first because it's shiny. They might even chew on it. But before long, they'll return to the comfort of the pacifier. You'd ask yourself, "Don't they understand what they have?" The answer is no—they don't.

This is what happens when you raise your thinking and language above those around you who aren't ready. The problem we face—not just in America, but globally—is a distorted value system. We often place high value on things that are meaningless, and chase after what can't truly fulfill us.

Jesus was once offered "all the kingdoms of the world" by Satan, in exchange for worship. But Jesus recognized that this was a lesser value compared to the eternal worth of obedience to

God. That same piece of gold could have purchased hundreds of pacifiers. The difference is perception. When you elevate your thoughts and spiritual maturity, the world doesn't change—your understanding does.

King Solomon said, *"There is nothing new under the sun."* If you walk into a dark house, you'll bump into furniture and stumble around. But when the lights come on, you see the same windows, paintings and details that were there all along. Illumination doesn't bring new things—it reveals what's always been there.

This awakening is necessary for you to receive deeper truths from God—especially concerning your money. God doesn't just hand out revelation randomly, although He desires to reveal Himself to all. He watched Saul for a long time before knocking him off that horse and revealing the light. That wasn't the first time God saw him.

Again, when the light begins to shine, you see the same things you've always seen, but now in a different way. And that's what illumination does.

Allow The Illumination to Come

This is your moment to be awakened—but you must *allow* the light to come. In **Genesis 1:3**, after the earth was found formless and void, God said, *"Let there be light."* The same is true for us. No one can make you see if you don't want to. We each have the freedom to hear—or not.

For a long time, I believed that anyone's life could change for the better if they just knew the right information. I now know that's not entirely true. True transformation begins when someone recognizes that something is off in their life—and they *seek out* a voice they trust to speak light into their spirit.

This Light is described in **Daniel 5:13–14**:

> *"Then was Daniel brought in before the king. And the king spake and said unto Daniel, 'Art thou that Daniel which art of the children of the captivity of Judah whom the king my father brought out of Jewry?*
>
> *I have even heard of thee, that the spirit of the gods is in thee, and that light and understanding and excellent wisdom is found in thee."*

The king wasn't referring to physical light—he was speaking of **insight, wisdom and spiritual**

intelligence. A higher intellect that perceives patterns and purpose.

More teachings on this will come in later chapters.

I'll also be picking on myself as we walk through my personal financial past to unlock some truths. "What was I thinking?" Consider your own life as we examine those who have always watched our money—and ask: *Why is it even important to them?*

Chapter 1: Father Knows Best

By the time a person reaches age eighteen, at least five figures are interested in their money. For many of us, there are only four. We're going to look over these to determine which of them may be absent.

The first figure your money is important to is God.

If you're anything close to how I was, you're probably asking yourself what does God have to do with my money? Don't we all make our money plans, then ask God to bless them? I mean, really, what does spirituality and my money have to do with each other? Surely, God isn't concerned with something as vain as money…could He?

Looking back, I can still remember the feelings and the beliefs that anyone who chooses to focus on money must be one who is filled with vanity and worldly wickedness. Many of us have experienced the negative emotions which appear to sit on our shoulders during church as the offering plate rolls around. Is it wrong to give? Are Pastors milking congregants out of all their money? Is God even cool with this?

Crash Course on Cash Flow

I grew up automatically paying 10% to the church I attended every week so it was not much of a challenge for me. I was maybe around age 20 when I fell short on my rent money one time. I had exhausted the payday loan thing and borrowed from everyone I loved--and a few I didn't.

Then it hit me: Wait! *Why not ask my church?* I was an unpaid drummer who showed up religiously, and I'd been tithing my whole life.

This seemed like a no-brainer. So, I contacted my uncle, the deacon, to set up a meeting.

I came into the church happy and upbeat, as usual. But the look on his face said it all—disappointment, even disgust. He rebuked me harshly, shocked that I'd allowed my finances to get so out of control. He went on and on about budgeting and responsibility. I was embarrassed.

What really blew me away was when he refused to simply give me the money. Instead, he wanted me to *repay* it. I remember quivering and asking, *'You mean...this is a loan?'* "Yes," he said. "And you'll make your payments on time, just like any other loan."

That transaction shook me to my core. It was as close to the only financial training I had ever received, and I was a zombie for about a year afterwards. It was the first time I had a first-hand look at paying into something for years only to never see anything in return. It fueled my struggle with keeping up with insurance payments on my car and many other financial obligations. Every time I got pulled over in my car my money situation worsened.

I'm not saying I was wronged or that my church was right, just describing my emotions and thinking at the time. Where do you stand on this?

I won't say that it's wrong or right to pay tithes. I'm interested in you understanding money regardless of whether you give or not. You'll make the right decision once you get it into your hands.

That experience gave me a crash course in what's known as '*cash flow*.' Money flows from one place to another—hence the term "liquidity." Your new mission is to learn how to tap into the cash flow in your life and divert some of it into your own reserves. The more you understand this process, the less financial struggle you'll face.

I didn't realize that after high school, I was still earning high school money—trying to live an adult life on it. I was completely unaware that God already had a financial system in place, built on seedtime and harvest. A divine blueprint for wealth. I didn't even know that *my* money mattered to *Him*.

I'll forever be grateful to God for delivering me from faulty financial beliefs. I was shaken awake at a men's conference in Darrow, Louisiana, where I finally saw in my Bible how God not only felt about *me*—but also about my *money*.

Before we go further, let's talk about identity—specifically, the identity crisis that clouds our understanding of who we are in God's eyes.

More Than a Friend--A Child

It's good to call yourself a friend of God. But it's even better to know you're His child— and as a bonus, to be a friend of your Father. The most important truth is this: You are His child.

Seeing yourself only as God's friend can also lead to the mistaken belief that you're on equal footing with Him. That can be offensive to God. *Why did You do it this way, God? Wouldn't it have been easier to do it my way?*

But when you see yourself as His child, you're more likely to trust His judgment—even when you don't understand it. Because you know He sees what you cannot. His ways are higher than ours. His thoughts, beyond our own.

In **Exodus 4:22,** God makes His heart clear. This is worth remembering:

> *"And thou shalt say unto Pharaoh, Thus saith the Lord, Israel is My son, even My firstborn. And I say unto thee, Let My son go, that he may serve Me..."*

Write this down:

"I am not a servant.
I am a child who serves."

____

____

____

A Relationship

It's an identity crisis because God doesn't want a transaction, He wants a relationship. He wants you to grab a cup of coffee, sit down and *talk to Him*.

Moses didn't have a clear picture of how God felt about him until that moment. But God spelled it out: *"You are My child."*

God often communes with us, but we typically are unclear about how He feels about us. But, here, from the mouth of God, He says, *'This is how I feel about you, and I want you to go and share this news with Pharaoh. You are My first-born child.'*

God is your Father. Your Dad. That's the foundation upon which every promise rests. If you don't see yourself as His child, then "serving" becomes a job. "Friendship" becomes conditional. But when you embrace the truth, *I am His child*—you unlock everything He has for you.

So, it's good that you're serving, but don't minimize the fact that He's your Dad. He wants you to get a cup of coffee to sit down with Him to talk. So yes, serve Him. But never forget: He's your Dad. Talk to Him.

My Money Is Important to God

In **Deuteronomy 28:11–12,** the Bible says:

> *"And the Lord shall make thee plenteous in goods, in the fruit of thy body, and in the fruit of thy cattle, and in the fruit of*

> *thy ground, in the land which the Lord sware unto thy fathers to give thee.*
>
> *The Lord shall open unto thee His good treasure, the heaven to give the rain unto thy land, in his season, and to bless all the work of thine hand."*

How much? See, listen to that, *'all the works of your hands.' That covers everything.*

It finishes *"and thou shalt lend unto many nations, and thou shalt not borrow."*

Wow!

So whether I like it or not, He says He will make me plenteous. Not metaphorically—*literally*. Every time I read this, I'm amazed: "All the work of your hands." That means everything I set out to do.

Then I read **Deuteronomy 8:18:**

> *"But thou shalt remember the Lord thy God: for it is He that giveth thee power to get wealth, that He may establish His covenant which He swore unto thy fathers, as it is this day."*

When I read that scripture in Darrow, Louisiana, It felt like I'd been part of some bizarre financial prank. The truth was hard to digest.

The Ability to Obtain Wealth

He gives me the power to obtain wealth—not just for my comfort, but to fulfill His covenant.

Still, I couldn't help but wonder: *How could God make me wealthy?*

The Word of God became a mirror. I didn't like what I saw. My lifestyle didn't reflect anything I had read. It was unsettling—this idea that God cared about my money and had something greater in mind. And then came the knockout blow from **Ecclesiastes 2:26:**

> *"For God giveth to a man that is good in His sight wisdom, and knowledge, and joy: but to the sinner He giveth travail, to gather and to heap up, that He may give to him that is good before God..."*

Translation? God cares most about *your ability to produce*—because understanding *how* to produce sustains what you receive.

Most people focus on receiving but never learn to maintain what they've gained. That's why they may get an expensive house but can't keep it. They achieve wealth but can't hold onto it. They never considered the monthly upkeep.

These scriptures confirmed it: Your money matters to God.

Roughly translated, knowing how to produce is what matters to God because it is the knowing which controls results. Most individuals arbitrarily focus more on receiving than on how to produce. This is why they often can get things but cannot hold on to them. It makes little sense to obtain a luxurious mansion for only two months because you've later realized how much it cost every month to hang on to it. As you can see, by these pieces of evidence, your money is definitely important to God.

BONUS QUOTE

For you

From the author!

"You should never be guilty of convincement or persuasion, only the uncovering of blinded eyes." — Charles H. Boxsley Jr.

Chapter 2: Even Satan Prays

Number Two: My Money Is Important to Satan

We've just seen how God is interested in your money. Now, here's number two: **Satan is also interested in your money.** We see this clearly in the life of Job —specifically in **Job 1:8–12.**

Imagine watching a movie, relaxing and unwinding. Meanwhile, behind the scenes, Satan and God are having a conversation—about you. Satan has his eyes on you, but he can't access you. So, what would any of us do when something feels too big to handle? We take it to the Lord in prayer.

Now consider this: **what if Satan is also *praying*—about you?** You might never have imagined that a seemingly silly little spiritual "game" could be used against you. You wouldn't have a clue.

We should all consider the strong possibility that there are things happening between us and God that Satan knows about—even if we don't. I suggest you live like that's true.

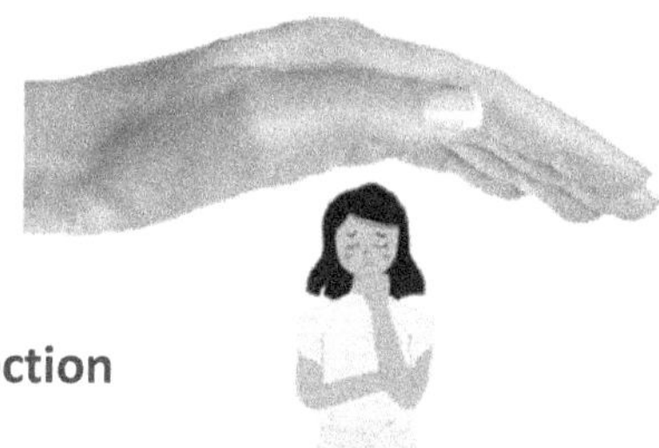

A Hedge of Protection

In **Job 1**, Satan asks, *"Have You not made a hedge around him?"* Wait—there's a hedge around me? Yes! He continues, *"Around his house,"* and just in case that's not clear enough: *"And around all that he has on every side?"*

We all know, what *all* means. But to underline the point further, Satan adds, *"You have blessed the work of his hands."* Satan isn't just targeting *you*—he wants to disrupt your *cash flow*.
This conversation between God and Satan happened without any human involvement. Just

two spiritual beings talking—no human input. To truly understand God's mind, we must observe Him in moments where He speaks without human interference.

We saw this with Abraham when he tried to negotiate with God to spare Sodom. God could have questioned why Abraham thought he could find 50 righteous people when He couldn't. But instead, God engaged with Abraham's reasoning, teaching him why the decision had to be made.

We rarely get a full glimpse into the mind of God. But when He speaks directly, that's His mind revealed. That's how He feels.

So far, we see both God and Satan are concerned with the productivity—or lack thereof—of your hands. But here's the detail I find most important: Satan had to get *permission* before he could even approach Job. As I said earlier, I believe this kind of exchange happens more often than we realize. So the next time you feel like Satan's on your back, remember—he had to get permission first.

That insight changed my financial life.

A bad habit I had to break was blaming Satan for all my financial misfortunes. Truth is, he wasn't involved nearly as much as I wanted to believe he was.

Games

In reality, I was just ignorant, unaware of the rules and principles of the game of cash flow.

Blaming the devil gave me an easy excuse. If he was responsible, then I didn't have to examine my own actions or my lack of financial IQ. But after learning about the hedge of protection around me, I couldn't use that excuse anymore.

Next, Satan tries a different tactic—he asks God to turn *against me*. In **Job 1:11**, Satan says, "But put forth Your hand now, and touch *all* that he has." Satan needs God's permission because he cannot act without God's Word. That's vital to understand—and to remember.

In 1997, I realized that the jobs I held were not enough to support my growing family. That pushed me to seek a skilled trade—a career. A few months later, I was enrolled in a heating, cooling and refrigeration program.

That decision changed my life. I met great friends and mentors and worked hard to be the best in my class. But despite all that, I remained financially stuck. Why? **Because I still didn't understand the financial principles that most businesses operate by**.

Satan doesn't *cause* ignorance, but he sure makes it seem harmless.

In business, there's a phrase: *more with less*. Depending on your role, that's either a good thing—or a terrible one.

Flames

After graduation, I was hired by several top HVAC companies in North America. Every

Monday, we had mandatory meetings. I thought they were just for updates. But at the end of each meeting, we'd all turn to a dry-erase board at the front of the room. Each technician's name was listed vertically, along with dollar amounts.

I was confused, weren't we all technicians? Why were we comparing *sales*?

The top earners were listed at the top... and there I was, at the bottom. It turns out, I wasn't hired just to be a service tech—I was also the *sales force*. I was their *"more with less."* Two roles, one paycheck.

In my mind, I became 40% service tech and 60% salesperson. Suddenly it made sense. They sent me to homes to do cleanings and change filters, while the top earners performed major repairs and /or replaced entire units.

Talk about flaming mad!

Those companies didn't care about the cleaning—I was there to *sell*. The cleaning was just my ticket through the front door. I was too honest—and too naïve—to realize it.

But what could I sell if everything the customer owned was brand new? I spent more time in interview rooms than I did actually working. Not every company operates this way, but if this sounds like your experience, it may explain why you feel so much pressure.

I had no idea I'd been hired to sell. It was part of the **unspoken rules of cash flow**—and no one told me.

Satan had one shot to take Job down. Why didn't he say, "Make him sick," or "Take a limb"? No. The *first* thing he targeted was the works of Job's hands—in other words, *his money*.

That's how important your money is to Satan.

So, when any of us walk around broke, we're living in alignment with Satan's goals—not God's. It's not about God keeping you from being greedy. **If you're greedy, Satan knows how to *put* money in your hands.** But if you have a heart to give and bless others, Satan works to *take* it out of your hands.

As Job's wealth increased, Satan asked God to strike everything he had—hoping Job would curse God in return.

So, could there be conversations happening about *you* while you sit back watching your favorite show? What about while you're in the middle of a heated argument with a coworker? Meanwhile, **the work of your hands is being targeted and attacked**.

You probably didn't realize your money was *that* important to Satan.

BONUS QUOTE
For you
From the author!

"Until business becomes your entertainment, you will continue to build the wealth of those who entertain you." — Charles H. Boxsley Jr.

Chapter 3: Say Uncle

So, there's God,—ruler of all—watching the works of your hands. Then there's Satan who wants God to touch all you have in a negative way. After the spirit realm, the next force in your life is your government. And yes, your money is important to them too.

Imagine you've finally found your long-sought perfect job. The hours are just right, the work is manageable, and the pay is enough to support you and your family.

But there's a catch: the job comes with an automatic spending partner who rarely shares your financial values or goals. When you want steak, they say you can't afford it. But when *they* want a new pair of shoes, there's magically enough money. They don't go to work with you, yet somehow, they get their cut of your paycheck *before* you do.

Whether the purchase is for you or for them, they want a percentage of every dollar spent in each transaction. After they receive their portion, you're left with the rest. But as soon as you walk into another store to make a different purchase—guess what--they want a percentage of that sale too. And before you get too far ahead of me, no, I'm not talking about your spouse or your child. How's that for a twisted game to find yourself in?

Baked into the System

Well, sorry to disappoint, but it's not a game. This is literally how taxes work— and it's baked into the system.

As I mentioned earlier, this system waited patiently for you to enter the workforce around age 16 or 18. Money that has already been taxed before you even get your check continues to be taxed every time you spend it. For every dollar you earn, less than a dime (give or take) gets used by you. They want you to start working legally as soon as possible so you can begin contributing to this government-run business model. Your money is very important to them. Let's look at an example in **Genesis 47:1–3:**

> *"Then Joseph came and told Pharaoh, and said, My father and my brethren, and their flocks, and their herds, and all that they have, are come out of the land of Canaan; and, behold, they are in the land of Goshen.*
>
> *And he took some of his brethren, even five men, and presented them unto Pharaoh. And Pharaoh said unto his brethren, What is your occupation? And they said unto Pharaoh, Thy servants are*

> *shepherds, both we, and also our fathers."*

Personally, I found this funny, there was no small talk. Pharaoh didn't greet them or offer water for their feet or animals. No *"It's good to see y'all"* or *"When did you arrive?"* He just got straight to business: *'What do you do for a living?'*

Taxes and More

There is one of many financial realities about our beloved planet I detest. That is the automatic assumption that everyone will be prepared to pay all their financial obligations by the time they reach adulthood.

Unfortunately, I grew up under extreme financial strain. In my mind, I thought I was doing well just by getting and keeping a job. I was so deep into my slumber, the moment I entered the working world, I didn't realize I also entered into the game of cash flow—with my automatic partner.

One of the rules of the game is that the government can charge you even more through fees and court filing costs that go well beyond what's withheld from your paycheck.

What does that mean? It means if someone begins driving while financially illiterate, they'll be overwhelmed by the countless regulations that govern the road.

From unpaid parking tickets to being pulled over without insurance; from expired tags to speeding tickets—it only takes a little irresponsibility for everything legal to come crashing down.

Yes, people should be more responsible—no argument there. Strive to obey traffic laws, by not blowing through stop signs; also known as *'rolling stops'* for instance. This would help reduce the flow of money from your hands to your automatic partner's.

But this chapter isn't about blaming the government. It's about waking up from your money slumber and understanding where the holes in your pockets are.

There's no benefit in being angry. You simply need to understand the *rules* of the game of cash flow. The system profits from ignorance. They, like many others in your life, have just created products because of your ignorance.

My mission is to help wake you up—because no one helped me until much later in my life. Once you start following the cash flow, you will see how government employees, i.e. police, fire, postal, trash and other service workers depend on your income and ability to pay your financial infractions.

Two Types of Jobs

Let's talk about work. There are essentially two types of jobs.

The first type depends purely on physical labor and basic effort. These are jobs anyone can do, with no special skills or qualifications required. I've had plenty of these.

They're problematic because they're among the lowest-paid roles within a company. By default, these jobs don't provide enough income to meet most people's needs and desires. They also create the illusion that you're bad with money—that you can't budget or that you spend wastefully. But in truth, your automatic partner is taking a cut of every check *before* you even see it. Then they tax that same money again and again every time you spend it.

The second type of job is skilled labor. This may not be shocking to some—but for someone financially asleep, the consequences can be huge. Skilled labor is value that lives *within* the individual. When you're absent from a skilled job, everyone notices. Skilled roles require critical thinking and the ability to adapt quickly to a variety of challenges. Because of this, they often pay more—mental demands outweigh physical effort.

Become Necessary

If you're currently in a "one-size-fits-all" job, I urge you to consider acquiring a skilled trade that requires problem-solving and thought. You need a skilled trade to become *necessary* to employers.

If I could give you a few ideas—whether you're male or female—I'd recommend looking into the commercial construction field: HVAC, plumbing, drywall, electrical, framing, sheet metal, etc. These trades have low barriers to entry and plenty of work. You can start as a helper. Just call a local trades staffing agency and they'll walk you through the next steps. (More on this later in the book.)

I wished someone had explained this to me around my 18th birthday. But if you're older, don't worry—this still applies.

Up to Date...

One of God's primary concerns is *the work of your hands—your income*.

The first thing Satan wants to attack is your *provision*.

And now, the first thing your government wants to know is: *How do you earn your money?* Or more bluntly: *How will you pay your taxes?*

Your money is highly important to them. They're concerned with how you'll contribute to the collective pot—one that a privileged few can access.

But don't worry—I'm not trying to scare you. I'm not anti-government. In fact, the whole picture of taxes isn't entirely negative.

For those interested, many states provide breakdowns of how taxes are spent. These categories, however, are often used by unethical actors to hide funding for personal projects, controversial agendas, or private gain.

Originally, taxes were designed to fund shared public expenses: postal services, police, fire departments, public schools and other communal programs.

So now, there are at least **three** forces watching what you do with the work of your hands: **God, Satan and the Government.**

Here's an example of how one city allocates its tax revenue:

By Jesse La Tour on July 10, 2020

General Fund Expenditures for 2020-21: $106,087,083

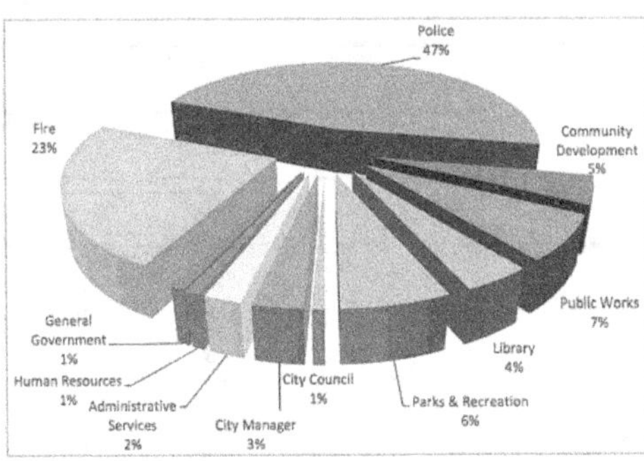

https://fullertonobserver.com/2020/07/10/council-approves-sales-tax-increase-ballot-measure/

BONUS QUOTE
For you
From the author!

"You are suffering not because of the lack of money, but because of the lack of knowledge. Knowledge is the cause. Money is the effect."

Chapter 4: My Creditors

In primitive times, merchants lost significant income because they only served individuals who had cash on hand or items to barter. I'm not talking about letting customers take products home and pay later without any record-keeping—records have always existed in some form.

The 30-Day Cycle

Eventually, merchants realized that most people don't have a lot of money at once—but they *will* over time. This insight gave birth to the 30-day cycle. Although it may have begun with good intentions, this cycle has become one of the most subtle forms of enslavement in modern society.

Another unwritten rule in the game of cash flow goes like this:

"Let customers just keep going to work every day. We'll continue producing products they can't afford."

This cycle traps us constantly purchasing items we're financially tied to in 30-day increments. It becomes a relentless battle over income we don't truly have. Let's face it—disposable income is a myth. Retirement is no longer defined by age; it's defined by the moment all your debts are paid off.

The risks vendors took in trusting customers to return and pay later led to the creation of insured purchases—transactions protected by law. Over the years, business communities have used various legal strategies to secure repayment for purchases or loans.

Two of the most common forms of legal protection used by creditors today are **judgments and garnishments**—both backed by laws and designed to protect your creditors.

Judgments

When I defaulted on loans or stopped making payments, the balance was added to my credit report. Sometimes it was just the remaining amount. Other times, like with a repossessed vehicle, I had to repay the full purchase price including the portion I had already paid.

Whenever I tried to move on financially without repaying old debts, they resurfaced like a ghost from the past, shouting:

"Hey there, remember me?"

It left me breathless. I would be forced to go all the way back and pay off that old debt before I could qualify for anything new.

Garnishments

Unbeknownst to me, my creditor went to court and told a judge I wasn't going to pay them. They both agreed to slap the debt on my credit report, making sure other lenders would see my irresponsibility and avoid me.

When I really got on their nerves, the creditor and the judge teamed up with my automatic partner, the government—and took the money directly from my paychecks. That's the power of **garnishments**.

When it first happened to me, I was furious—especially with the HR lady at my job. My check was short, and I couldn't pay my current bills. But the truth was: **they were right, and I was**

wrong. I had zero financial education growing up, no warnings, no lessons about the rules of cash flow. So yes, I was shocked to learn how important my money was to my creditors.

Body Attachments

In collections, a **writ of body attachment** is basically an arrest warrant. If someone fails to appear in court after being summoned to address a debt, the court can issue this writ and haul them in.

For Bible readers, this shows up in **2 Kings 4:1**:

> *"Now there cried a certain woman of the wives of the sons of the prophets unto*

> *Elisha, saying, 'Thy servant my husband is dead; and thou knowest that thy servant did fear the Lord: and the creditor is come to take unto him my two sons to be bondmen."*

This story hit me hard. It showed just how important my money was to my creditors. Important enough to come to my house and take my kids to work off my debt. **Creditors are proactive**. They project years ahead.

There's a philosophy I adopted early in adulthood:

"The only problem with me paying my bills is... that I'm the one paying them."

Funny? Maybe.
But let's dig deeper.

Bills exist because of a lack of money and because we decided to work a job. They're born from financial insufficiency. When we need something, we can't afford, creditors step in and say: *"You can have it now if you pay it off in 30-day cycles."*

It sounds reasonable until you look under the hood.

The main job of a creditor is to keep you locked in 30-day payment cycles as long as you're employed. This gives them time to pay off their own debt, overhead, raw goods, etc.--because **promissory notes and receivables are as good as cash** to them.

Their goal?
Future revenue.

In Perpetuity

After getting denied for a basic loan by traditional banks—couldn't even get one for a bologna sandwich—I went to a "buy here, pay here" auto dealer.

We were both excited about the deal. I got the keys and drove off. Each time I made a payment, I felt good knowing I was getting closer to the final one. But around the last four payments, the dealer noticed the car wasn't looking too good anymore. He suggested I trade it in for something newer, more reliable.

I'll admit—he was good. He almost had me. But then it clicked: **I was in a game**.

He never wanted me to finish paying off that car. He wanted me in **perpetual debt**; a continuous customer recycling vehicles through me forever. That realization made me furious. I hate being taken advantage of. But I had to stay calm and shift into learning mode. Another fast, hard lesson in the game of cash flow.

I also learned that if I ever rebelled—by stealing or vandalizing, for example—creditors would just raise prices or cut employee hours to recover the loss. **They don't pay their own expenses**. Their employees and customers do.

That's why I shake my head when people rob or loot stores. A few months later, they'll be back in that same store complaining about the $10 gallon of milk. If you think that's how you hurt a business, you're dreaming.

Your money is too important to your creditors. They will always find a way to recover.

BONUS QUOTE

For you

From the author!

"When you allow your eyes to focus on results, you'll never improve on the causes of results."

Chapter 5: My Money?

As I mentioned earlier, I struggled to understand why I could never seem to hold onto anything I worked hard for—whether it was repossessed or returned prematurely. Meanwhile, most people around me rarely lost anything and seemed to continually enjoy the fruits of their labor. It wasn't until I got older that I began to see things more clearly.

Consistency

One glaring difference between myself and others growing up was *consistency*. Almost every part of their lives followed a routine. I'm not saying their lives were perfect by any means, but in hindsight, I now recognize how they embraced regular schedules—mealtimes, homework, bedtimes, and so on. Many were also actively involved in after-school sports or other extracurricular activities.

This made them ideal candidates for the workforce. As we all know, consistency may seem boring, but like a steady drip of water, it can ultimately bore right through concrete. It builds long-term stability.

A hard truth I had to face was that the chaos and inconsistency of my upbringing made it difficult for me to maintain employment. Growing up around substance abuse and frequently moving between families and schools, I didn't have the stability and structure that most jobs require.

I became someone who was rarely on time and struggled to stick with repetitive tasks—hardly a recipe for keeping a job, a car or an apartment that demanded regular payments.

Other routine financial obligations like insurance, vehicle tags and traffic violations were equally disastrous in my chaotic world. These responsibilities only accelerated my descent into debt and poverty.

It is far easier to handle these challenges when you've lived in the same house, attended the same schools and experienced stability growing up. Most kids I knew never had to endure having their utilities shut off at home.

Is Your Money Important to You?

Eventually, I found myself much like the woman in **2 Kings 4:1**. I owed a mountain of debt while sleeping through a financial slumber.

Anyone observing me might have assumed that money wasn't important to me. But the truth was, I found it easier to blame everything *outside* myself for my financial struggles.

One day, I had to ask myself—point blank—as I now ask you:

"Is your money important to you?"

Here are a few things I've learned about myself and my money:

1. *Pay God first—10% in tithes.*

2. *Recognize how easily Satan can entertain you out of your money.*

As long as I was shopping, watching movies or living recklessly, Satan had no need to interfere. I fell among the crowds in my city and lived riotously (metaphorically). Little by little, I was being entertained out of my future.

3. *Understand that the government is your automatic financial partner.*

They always want their taxes. The rules to the game of cash flow allow the government to spend my money however they choose—while I'm left holding the bag. It makes it hard for me to believe him when he says he wants me. I've got a strange feeling that it's my taxes he really wants, right?

4. *Creditors were waiting for me to turn 16 or 18.*

They hoped I'd be well-trained to join their 30-day payment matrix. My money matters to them. They may not come after my children to work off my debts like in the old days, but I'm still on their balance sheets—and that's just fine with them.

This brings us to our final number 5.

5. ***Is your money important to you?***

If everyone else has a financial stake in your life *except you*, it's no surprise you're stuck in chaos.

Time to Blame Ourselves

The woman in **2 Kings 4** had spent years not valuing her money. Who knows how old she was? She had all that time to improve her financial situation—but didn't. Only after her husband died did she wake up and seek a way out.

To her credit, she found someone—a prophet—who showed her the path forward. This aligns with **Jeremiah 5:1**, which says:

> *'Run ye to and fro through the streets of Jerusalem, and see now, and know, and seek in the broad places thereof, if ye can find a man, if there be any that executeth*

judgment, that seeketh the truth; and I will pardon it.'

Her life changed the moment she admitted her role in her financial troubles and sought help. She found someone who could speak truth and wisdom into her life. If you allow me, I'd like to be that person for you. To help awaken the unique gift inside you that's been lying dormant. The world is waiting for your contribution. Again, I ask:

"Is your money important to you?"

Twenty Years-Plus, Left

Yes, this book is about *you*! You are number five. Have you lived this long without truly valuing your money? Will you wait for a crisis to come along before you make a change?

If you're still reading, that means I have your attention. This is your shaking. If you keep sleeping through life, you'll start justifying inaction with your age or other distractions. I challenge you to live each day as if you have at least *twenty more years* left to create change.

Like the woman in our story, you now face a decision. Either you'll go home and find something of value to share with the world—or life will keep taking from you, one thing at a time. Let me echo the words of the prophet:

'You need a product.'

A product gives others a reason to pay you. And that may be exactly what's missing in your life.

The Seed...Inside and Out 

You must give people a reason to exchange their money with you—*beyond just your labor*. A job means you're selling your physical strength—the *shell* of your seed. But a product allows you to sell your ideas—your *inner value*.

The shell of a seed is to be discarded. You must sell the *nutrition* of your intellect. Every 30 days, you owe at least six people money. How many people owe *you* money every 30 days?

But First...

Earlier, I mentioned skilled trades. They offer a low barrier to entry, especially when starting as a helper or laborer. For commercial construction, reach out to a local trades staffing agency. They'll guide you.

Adult bills require adult jobs. You'll need enough income to do two things:

1. *Pay your current bills.*

2. *Have enough left over to acquire assets.*

Your Ultimate Goal

Don't pay bills with your hard-earned paycheck. Instead, use job income to buy financial education—books, courses, and resources.

You must learn the vocabulary of the new financial "land" you'll be living in. This is key to understanding financial opportunities and to keep up with money conversations and decisions that impact you.

When you constantly ask, *"What should I invest my money in?"*—that's a sign that more reading is needed. That question only summons people who look for easy ways out of their financial troubles. Your money plus their ignorance equals two broke fellows.

Investments aren't good or bad. The investor is. Your past struggles and successes are key to discovering what investments fit *you*.

Let your past pains pay you back. Did you spend years working on cars? Maybe your passion for juicing turned into perfect recipes. Do friends constantly ask you for workout advice?

Your freedom lies in your bondage.

The very thing that seemed to keep you stuck may be what God uses to elevate you. You know what your passion is. Pray for divine direction, then act as doors begin to open and others close.

Create products and let your customers pay your bills. That's what the woman in **2 Kings** did with her sons—they produced oil to sell and paid off their debts and lived on the rest.

So... What's in Your House?

It's time to awaken from your financial slumber and show the world just how important your money is to you!

BONUS QUOTE
For you
From the author!

"The purpose of money is to be sown as a seed for a money harvest!"

REFLECTION:

Write down your thoughts now that your eyes have been opened.

www.ingramcontent.com/pod-product-compliance
Lightning Source LLC
LaVergne TN
LVHW020325220926
848484LV00001BB/4
* 9 7 9 8 9 9 8 5 7 7 6 1 1 *